THE
Archive Photographs
SERIES

YORK

York Library staff pose for a group photograph, c. 1929. the older gentleman seated in the middle of the middle row is Arthur Finney who was City Librarian from 1929-1935. He worked at both the original library in Clifford Street which opened in 1893 and in the new purpose-built library in Museum Street which was completed in 1927. Next to him is Raymond Doherty who succeeded him and remained City Librarian until 1959.

THE
Archive Photographs
SERIES

YORK

Compiled by
Amanda Howard

CHALFORD

First published 1995
Copyright © Amanda Howard, 1995

The Chalford Publishing Company
St Mary's Mill, Chalford,
Stroud, Gloucestershire, GL6 8NX

ISBN 0 7524 0331 1

Typesetting and origination by
The Chalford Publishing Company
Printed in Great Britain by
Redwood Books, Trowbridge

*In memory of my Father-in-law
Alban Howard.*

The market in Parliament Street in the early 1960s, before its final closure in 1964.

Contents

Acknowledgements

I would like to thank all those who have donated material to York Central Library's collection in the past and the following who have kindly lent me their own photographs for this book:

Ian Clough, Herbert Dixon, Douglas Ewbank, Ann Harding, John Leedham, Patrick Oldfield, Yvonne Pethullis, David Poole, Quentin Smallpage and Averil Webster.

Thanks also to Sue Richmond for the long term loan of her VCH.

Special thanks go to Hugh Murray who lent me photographs and also gave me the benefit of his vast knowledge of York.

Introduction

York's beauty is world famous and photographers have attempted to capture it on film since the beginning of the photographic age. As a result, a comprehensive visual record of the past 150 years of York's history now exists. York Central Library is fortunate to have built up an extensive collection of photographs dating from the earliest images produced in the 1840s up to the present day. This has been achieved largely through gratefully received donations and it is hoped that it will continue to grow. The library aims to increase and preserve this collection and make it available to anybody who wishes to use it. Here a small part of its contents are reproduced to give a glimpse of the diversity that it contains.

Selecting photographs to include from the library's collection which numbers over nine thousand items was a difficult choice. The guiding principle was to include as many as possible that have not been published before and to show not only the famous views of the centre of York but to venture into the suburbs which have often been neglected in preference to the central area. A further aim was to show those that focus on the experiences of York's people rather than concentrating solely on the building. To achieve this, photographs from outside the library's collection have occasionally been used and I would like to record my thanks to those individuals who kindly lent me their own photographs.

The immediate impression when looking at old photographs of York is one of surprise at how little some of the scenes have changed over the years. The Minster at the heart of the city and streets around it, such as The Shambles, Petergate and Stonegate have a timeless quality and would be instantly recognisable now to their photographers. However a closer look reveals that York is not just a city of great architectural beauty where time has stood still, but the home of a community which has witnessed many changes.

Before the birth of photography, the people lived and worked inside the walls. Beyond the bars, there was very little development and what there was clung to the approach roads to the city, such as Blossom Street and Bootham. Outside the walls was open countryside with a place like Holgate, now an integral part of York, a rural township with its own identity. The presence of industrial activity and housing for all social classes, including overcrowded terraces for the poorest of the community, within the city centre is a side of York that is rarely portrayed, but there is evidence of its existence in the photographs. However as York's population has increased and industry evolved, the city has expanded into the suburbs. This has resulted in a change in the role of the centre, away from its traditional uses towards shopping, entertainment and tourism.

One major factor that triggered this change was the coming of the railways with the first station opening in 1839. It quickly became York's largest employer and the need to accommodate its workforce led, for example, to the development of Holgate as a suburb. They also stimulated the city's industrial growth, particularly the confectionery industry. Joseph Terry and Co. expanded in the 1850s and the workforce of Rowntree's soared from 100 in 1879 to over 4,000 in 1909. Originally their factory was in Tanners Moat, but in 1890 Joseph Rowntree took the decision to move out of the city centre and he bought land on Haxby Road for his new suburban factory. Consequently housing and services developed around it for the workers and a community was created.

York Corporation, as well as the city's main industrial players, influenced the growth of the suburbs. They began a programme of clearing the inner-city slums and rehousing their inhabitants on land outside the walls. Building on the Tang Hall estate, for example, began in 1919 for those made homeless by the clearance of terraces in Walmgate. Others followed such as Chapelfields after Acomb became part of York in 1937, thus further extending the city. Today as the newly-created York District Council prepares to take control of the Greater York area, the city continues to expand its boundaries.

One
The Historic Centre

A group of children enjoy the beauty of Dean's Park in the 1930s.

The Princess of Wales Yorkshire Regiment march past York Minster as part of the Military Sunday Parade, 1911. They were held annually, at the suggestion of Dean Purey-Cust, as a tribute to General Gordon who died at Khartoum in 1885. The first one took place in York in 1892.

Duncombe Place, c. 1905. The Boer War memorial was a new addition to Duncombe Place erected in 1905. The railings have now been replaced by a wall and the trees have grown giving a less open outlook.

What is most striking about this view of Stonegate in c. 1890 is how little it has changed over the years. The Star Inn's advertising board has spanned the street since 1733, bringing its hidden, courtyard position to the attention of passing shoppers.

Newgate looking towards Kings Square. The church is Holy Trinity which was demolished in 1937. It had been in decline for many years; in the 1890s it was used as a pound for sheep awaiting slaughter. Despite this, a campaign was led by the Yorkshire Archaeological and York Architectural Society to save it. Writing in 1931, they stated that it was one of the best seen of the York churches when walking down Petergate and a bare and ugly gap would be left if it was demolished.

Kings Square, 1950s. As the years have gone by, the open space left by the demolition of Holy Trinity church has become valued as a place to rest and, today, be entertained by one of the many street performers.

The deliverymen have stopped outside the Eagle and Child Inn in The Shambles, c. 1895. In this year, they would have had the choice of three other hostelries to quench their thirst, The Globe, The Neptune and The Shoulder of Mutton. The Eagle and Child continued trading until 1925, outlived only by The Globe. Its closure in 1936 ended the long tradition of pint-pulling in The Shambles.

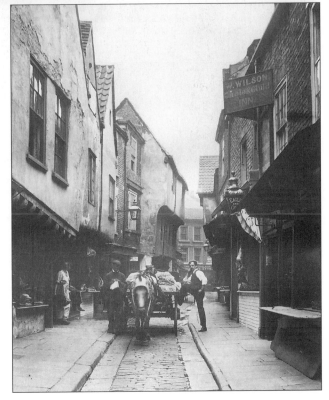

The photographer has perfectly caught the sun highlighting the ancient buildings in The Shambles. The mood is one of tranquillity and leisure in this usually busy street.

The Little Shambles, bustling with activity. Only a few of the buildings at the top of the street remain. The rest were demolished to make way for Newgate Market in 1954.

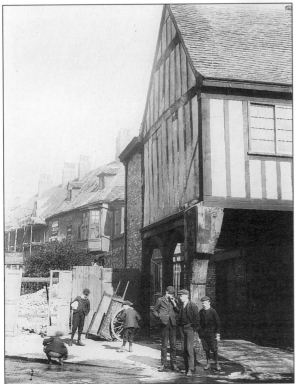

College Street showing the gateway from Goodramgate during the construction of Deangate in 1903. The timber-framed building the boys are standing in front of was originally destined to be sacrificed as part of the Deangate scheme. However it was bought by Frank Green, who was renovating St Williams College, and as a result it was saved from demolition.

Lady Row, Goodramgate, 1963. These are the oldest domestic buildings in York and were known as Lady Row as early as 1548. Opposite is a rare sight for present-day residents - car parking in the heart of the city centre! A concrete arcade of shops was built where the cars are standing soon after the photograph was taken.

Goodramgate looking towards Church Street, c. 1910. Horse-power was still very much in evidence in the York streets at this date, despite the arrival of motor-driven vehicles. There is also a hand-pulled dust cart on the right-hand side of the road.

The corner of Newgate and Jubbergate, c. 1924. Muir's cycle shop was competing for business in 1924 with forty-six others throughout the city, selling cycles and carrying out repairs, an indication of the popularity of cycling which continues today but not with so many retail outlets!

New Street in the 1940s. The Tudor Cafe opened in 1898 on the top floor of Barton's confectioners and served teas until its closure in 1957. After an absence of thirty-four years, it reopened in September 1991, under the auspices of its new owners, Liberty of London.

Tanner's Moat, c. 1854. This famous view of the Minster from the bar walls has undergone many changes. Nestling next to the bar walls stand some railway vehicles, a reminder that the station was originally between Toft Green and the walls. Lendal Bridge has not yet been erected and what is now Station Rise is crammed with houses.

Lendal Bridge from Manor Shore. The City Council took the decision to build a bridge to replace the ferry service in June 1857. The work started but, tragically, the partially completed bridge collapsed on 27 September 1861 killing seven men. This proved to be opportune for some who petitioned the council to change the design. They were successful and the original girder bridge was abandoned. It was rescued from the river and sold to the Scarborough Corporation to form part of the Forge Valley Bridge. New plans were adopted and the present bridge was formally opened in November 1863.

Pedestrians and a few vehicles cross Lendal Bridge, c. 1905. The balustrade was raised to its present height by the addition of an extra row of quatrefoils in 1910, when the bridge was strengthened for the electric trams.

Rougier Street. The spire of All Saints, North Street, visible since the Middle Ages, is the only landmark that can be recognised today. The street has been considerably widened and the appearance of the York Industrial and Equitable Society in 1899, later the Co-op, swept away the buildings in the distance.

Rougier Street, c. 1959. There are three striking differences between this photograph and what we see today. Firstly the General Accident Building has not yet been built, secondly, the row of terraces are no longer standing. Numbers 1-14 were acquired by Leedhams in 1962 and demolished to allow them to expand their garages. Thirdly the building housing the York Hire and Drive Company has been considerably shortened. Originally it was a horse repository providing stabling for 200 horses. It opened in 1884 and was once named as one of the ugliest buildings in Europe!

The corner of Market Street and Coney Street, 1878. Ellerington's, a tobacconist, only occupied this site for a short time between 1876 and 1879. Burton's now stands here.

High Ousegate. The gabled building has now disappeared and Habitat stands here. Walkers Milliners has been emptied ready for demolition. The boy is standing outside Pickerings, then a bookshop, toy shop and decorating business. When it moved out of High Ousegate in 1958 after trading there since 1857, the two main stands of the business separated, with the bookshop opening in The Shambles and the toy shop in Minster Gates. Both are still trading today.

Pavement, 1910. The appearance of this street was radically altered following the decision to create a new street, Piccadilly, in 1911. Melias Tea Stores, Braimes and Isaac Poad next door were all casualties of this scheme. In 1955, Pavement was cut through again to make another new street, Stonebow. This time The Old George Hotel was the casualty.

Piccadilly, 2 March 1912. The City of York Engineers Department captures the breakthrough from Parliament Street and the start of the new road.

An abutment for the new bridge on the south side of the River Foss, 21 April 1911, required for the creation of Piccadilly. The workmen take a break to pose for the camera and behind them are some of the terraces which were pulled down to make the road. The timber-framed building is The Red Lion Pub now in Merchantgate which was formed at the same time as Piccadilly.

Two
Living in the City

Archers in Aldwark, 1940s. The boys from the community living in and around Aldwark enjoy a time-honoured game of bows and arrows.

Ogleforth looking towards Goodramgate and beyond to Aldwark. The children look very well dressed and the 1891 census returns reveal that it was a well-to-do street with households having several servants and often 'living on their own means'.

These houses in Swinegate and Finkle Street look in a poor state of repair when this photograph was taken in the late 1890s, but it was not until 1936 that they were the subject of a clearance order.

Garden Place, Hungate, December 1912. Hungate was one of the first areas to be targeted by the city council for slum clearance following the 1890 Housing Act. In a report by the medical officer in 1908, it was condemned for a number of reasons including the high proportion of back-to-back terraces, the general dilapidation of the houses, deficient water supply and closet accommodation, unpaved yards and overcrowding.

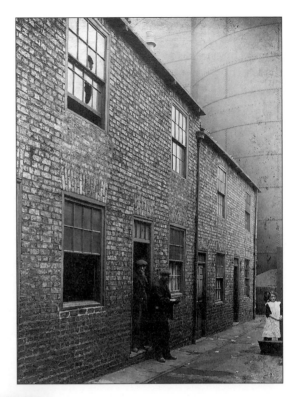

Nos. 18 and 20 Garden Place, Hungate, 1912. One of the serious defects that the medical officer drew attention to in his report was the narrowness of the streets which made the houses ill-ventilated and dark. Garden Place was 435 feet long but the average width was only sixteen feet and seven inches. He stated that as a result of these conditions, which were exacerbated by the smallness of the houses and the overcrowding, their inhabitants were permanently tired and cadaverous with a great disposition to resort to drink.

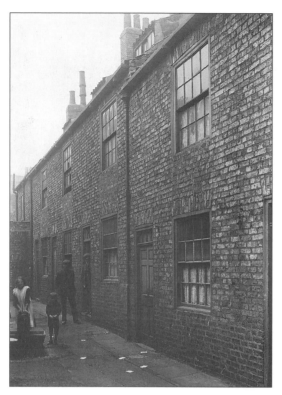

Bellerby's Yard, Hungate, 1911.

Bradley's Buildings, Hungate, 1911.

Arthur Hemmens stands outside his shop in North Street where he was still serving at the ripe old age of 90. A well-known character and collector of local items of interest especially relating to the North Street area, he was interviewed by the *Yorkshire Gazette* in 1941. The article concluded with the statement that Arthur was 'a nonagenarian grocer to whom it is a delight to listen'. He died three years later at the age of 94.

North Street was once filled with houses on both sides of the street. This is the White House c. 1900, which along with many other properties, stood on the site of what is now the Riverside Gardens.

A delightful picture of children peering into Hemmen's corner shop, North Street. Cissie followed in her father's footsteps and ran the shop into her advancing years. It finally closed in 1968 after a daylight robbery raid which left Cissie deeply shocked and no longer willing to continue. She retired to an old people's home and died in 1984 at the age of 98.

Opposite: Trinity Lane housed a working class community and had four squares and streets leading off it. One of these, Florence Row, was occupied in 1902 by a NER porter, two labourers, a machinist and a chimney sweep. The building advertising *The News of the World* was both a newsagents and a confectioners and the proprietor in 1902 was John Hall.

Prospect Gardens, Bishophill Junior was one of the many garden squares that could be found in terraced areas of York. It has been replaced by Oliver House which opened in 1965 as an old people's home.

Three
Shopping in the Centre

The Shambles showing some of the butchers shops, for which it is famous, open for business. The displays of meat on the medieval benches or 'shamels' after which the street is named, would not pass today's strict health and safety standards!

Petergate, 1965. Ernest Precious built up York's well-loved toy and model shop in the interwar years, beginning as a toy wholesaler in Swinegate. The Petergate store was established by the outbreak of the Second World War and continued trading until November 1987. Next door is Scott's butchers which was founded in 1889 and run by three generations of Scotts until July 1978. Although no longer in the family, it is still open and continues to be famous for its pork pies!

34

Sadd's Fruit Shop, Goodramgate, 1939-45. Wartime queues outside the greengrocers as rationing hits York.

The expression on the face of the gentleman emerging from Sadd's complete with purchases, contrasts with the look of anxiety on the face of the girl still queuing.

Banks & Sons, Stonegate, c. 1910. In 1885 an advertisement in the *Yorkshire Gazette* boasted that Banks had the largest music stock in England. Originally trading further down Blake Street, they moved to the prestigious corner position with Stonegate in c. 1910 and remained there until 1985 when they opened in new premises in Lendal.

Chapman & Wilson, stationers and booksellers opened at 36 Coney Street in December 1883. It remained in business until 1957.

Leak & Thorp, Coney Street, 1911. In 1947 they celebrated their centenary beginning life in Parliament Street and moving into Coney Street in 1869. During its 139 year history it underwent many refits, including a major one in 1981-2 after being taken over by Joplings of Sunderland. It closed in March 1987 with Hamley's toy shop initially taking over the site.

J.H. Wilson, drapers, Pavement, 1910. Their premises, Herbert House, at this time did not have the familiar sag that it has today. This has been caused by the volume of modern traffic using the road. Its fine beams have now been exposed.

Outside Hunter & Smallpage, Goodramgate, c. 1911. Thomas Hunter opened his furnishing store in 1875 and was soon joined by Benjamin Smallpage. They remained in Goodramgate until 1986 and now trade from premises in Micklegate. In the early days all the furniture and upholstery was manufactured in the shop with the craftsmen starting work at 6.00am and walking home for breakfast at 8.00am.

Hunter & Smallpage, Feasegate branch. Following a merger with Bellerby's furnishings and upholstery business in 1921, the company had two city centre outlets. This store was hit by an incendiary bomb during the Second World War and closed shortly after the war.

The interior of Hunter & Smallpage showing the linen and glassware departments which together with lighting and china were added to the range in the 1950s. The chairs are for customers who would be shown the linen by the sales assistants, a more enjoyable and relaxing shopping experience than that of today.

This view of Spurriergate was taken as recently as 1980, however Burton's is the only shop of those that can be seen which is still trading today.

Boyes Remnant Warehouse, Ousebridge, 1906-1911. W. Boyes' York Shop followed his success in Scarborough opening in 1906. It dominated Ousebridge until its closure early in 1982. The store was bought by a Leeds property firm with plans to divide into four separate units, testifying to its enormous size. After a four year absence, Boyes returned to York opening in Goodramgate in May 1987.

G.W. Harding. High Ousegate entrance. Harding's linen and furnishings store was founded in 1883 and remained in the family until its closure in 1974. The premises were bought by Terence Conran who personally flew in to look at them and instantly decided to buy. The amazing Leaning Tower of Pisa display made from napkins was created by the first G.W. Harding for the annual window dressing competition organised by the city council. It came second with the judges agreeing that if it hadn't been leaning, it would have scooped first place! In disgust, Mr Harding sent the errand boy to collect the award.

G.W. Harding, Coppergate entrance, c. 1908. This was the first large building that Shepherds, the York firm of builders, erected. It was commissioned by G.W. Harding and completed in 1908. The magnificent decoration is very evocative of the art nouveau period. The stunning ladies are made of Burmantoff's pottery manufactured near Leeds.

The market in Parliament Street in 1889. Parliament Street was created by an Act of Parliament granted in 1833. This was sought as a measure to ease the congestion in Pavement

where the general market had been held previously. The new street hosted its first market in June 1836.

The meat, fish and poultry section of the Newgate Market in September 1961. The transfer of the market from Parliament Street was gradual. The fish stalls opened in 1955 but the general market was not up and running until April 1964.

Four

Walmgate
and Beyond its Bar

Looking down Walmgate from within the bar, May 1907. Behind the row of shop fronts was a honeycomb of terraced streets, alleys and courts. Walmgate was the main area of Irish settlement in York following the potato famines of the 1840s and their occupation gave it a unique character.

Albert Street, Walmgate, was one of the complex of terraced streets that were to be found within the bar. Many were condemned in *A Report into the Sanitary Conditions in the Walmgate Area*, published in 1914. It found a large number of houses to be dilapidated, overcrowded, damp and without 'free access of light and air'. Albert Street, along with Navigation Road, was singled out as been particularly narrow. It was demolished in 1919 and the residents were rehoused on the Tang Hall estate.

Hill's Yard, Walmgate, 1933.

Navigation Road, Walmgate, 1933. The flats which now stand in this road were awarded a prize as part of the 1951 Festival of Britain celebrations.

An aerial photograph of the Tang Hall estate showing Melrosegate, the Derwent Valley Railway and St Hilda's church in the centre foreground, 1972. The council took the decision to buy land in Tang Hall in 1915 to rehouse those made homeless by the slum clearances which started in 1919. By 1925, 367 houses had been built for the 805 residents of only five Walmgate streets.

The approach to Walmgate Bar from Hull Road, c. 1940. In 1644 the area outside Walmgate Bar was thronged with Parliamentary forces besieging the city. The royalists within the walls held out until after the Battle of Marston Moor, but the Parliamentarians had some success in breaching the defences at Walmgate following an attack on the bar by cannon and mines. It was rebuilt immediately after the end of the civil war.

The Tam O'Shanter pub in Lawrence Street, 1934, was given this name between 1851 and 1854 after a famous racehorse of the time.

The workforce of Sheppee Engineering outside their workshop in James Street, c. 1910. They were considered to be one of the leading steam-driven vehicle makers of their time. They became a limited Company in 1918 and were rescued from receivership in 1993 when they became known as Sheppee International Ltd. They continue in York today.

The Sheppee Steam Lorrie piggybacks a Sheppee car to the workshop for repair, c. 1911. This image gives justification to the claim of R. A. Whitehead writing in 1979 that 'Sheppee's vehicles were brilliant yet temperamental'!

Members of St. Lawrence Church process down Lawrence Street in honour of the feast of Corpus Christi, June c. 1930. There have been two churches of St Lawrence. The original one was taken down between 1881 and 1883 and the tower and doorway can still be seen in the grounds of the present church, which was consecrated in May 1883 by the Archbishop of York.

The York Industrial and Equitable Society, Melrosegate branch. The society was founded in 1859 and was the forerunner of the York Co-operative Society.

Mr Harrison, the butcher, stands outside the butchers department of the Melrosegate Co-op in 1930.

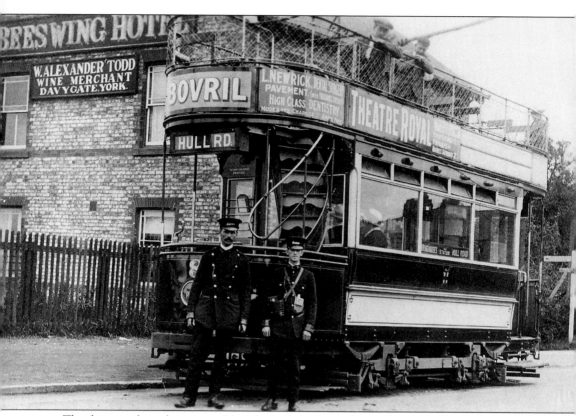

The driver and conductor stand beside their tram outside the Beeswing Hotel, the last stop on Hull Road. The line opened in June 1914.

Some of the first pupils to attend Fishergate Primary School following its opening in 1895. It was designed for the York School Board by Walter Brierley, the York architect who was also responsible for Poppleton Road, Scarcroft and Park Grove schools. It is thought to be on the site of the medieval church of St Helens Fishergate.

The corner of Grange Street and Fulford Road, 1934. The shop on the corner is an off-licence and the photograph is one of a collection of all the premises throughout the city owned by John Smith Breweries. This unique record was taken by Edwin Lofthouse in 1934.

A soldier stands outside the cavalry barracks on Fulford Road. They were built in 1795-96 as part of William Pitt's barrack-building programme which was launched in 1792. The last horses left in January 1939 when the 15/19th Hussars were equipped with armoured cars. York Police Station now stands on the site.

Five
Without Bootham Bar

Bootham Bar is the entrance to the city from the Great North Road. The barbican was taken down in 1832 when the whole bar was threatened with removal. Thankfully this plan was dropped after opposition from conservationists and with the Minster as its backdrop, it is one of the best-known views of York. This photograph was taken before 1889 when the steps up the side of the bar were added.

Gillygate in the early 1940s. The criss-cross pattern in the window above the shop canopy is tape, put on during World War Two to minimise the impact of breaking glass in a bombing raid.

Clarence Street looking towards Gillygate in the 1900s. The gateway which the two ladies are walking past, is the entrance to Clarence House. Opposite the row of bay-fronted terraces set back from the road stand on what is now Union Terrace car park.

A tea party to celebrate the opening of the Clarence Gardens Pavilion on 16 July 1913. It was organised by the Clarence Gardens Bowling Club for thirty veterans who frequented the gardens.

Bootham decorated with flags in honour of the Duke of York, later George V, who received the Freedom of the City, October 1893. On this visit he also opened the first public library in York which was in Clifford Street.

A view from Railway Walk in 1902 across the roof tops to St Olave's church. The photographer is standing between Walker Street and Clayton Street, and we see the back of Frederic Street and beyond to Marygate. These terraces were demolished in 1973 and Marygate car park was built. Ironically the council is currently planning to close the car park and once again use the land for housing.

Another view down Railway Walk from Bootham showing the ends of all the terraced rows that were crammed into the small area which is now the car park. On the right hand side of the pathway are the backs of the advertising boards seen in the previous photograph and on the opposite side, advertisements have been pressed into the concrete strips which run the entire length of the alley. Before the Town and Country Planning Act of 1948 which gave the council powers of regulation, advertisements literally covered any available space throughout the city.

This row of shops in Bootham between Bootham Cresent and Grosvener Terrace would have satisfied most everyday needs in the 1940s. From left to right is Thomas Tyerman Sturdy, the chemist, Alfred Hannon, fruiterer – member of a family who had a number of such businesses in York, the most famous of which was probably their fruit and vegetable shop in Stonegate – Edmund Moat, grocer and Coastal Fisheries selling fish and game.

This was the forerunner of the present Burton Stone Inn which was built in 1896. The stone it refers to is the boundary stone which can still be seen today. It is said that since the rebuilding of the pub, the stone was moved onto brewery property for which privilege the city pays a rental of one pence a year!

Burton Stone Windmill was also known as Clifton or Lady Windmill. There is a mention of a mill in this vicinity as early as the late fourteenth century. In 1807, the postmill was offered for sale in the *York Courant* and described as a freehold windmill with a stable and outbuilding. Also included in the sale were the millstones and sails.

Hudsons's Yard, Clifton was on the south side of the green. Its rural setting is a reminder that even within living memory, Clifton was a village outside York.

Cottages in Clifton, 1922. They stood between Burton Stone Lane and The Green and had been thatched. At this time they were owned by Mr S. Holtby, a joiner and cabinet maker, and before this they had been farm houses.

Flooding on Clifton Green, October 1892. This photograph was taken by a master at St Peter's from his dressing room window. The crowd watching the scene are St Peter's boys wearing their Sunday top hats. On this occasion the Ouse rose to 15 ft and 8 in above normal, following forty hours of rain.

Six
Outside Monk Bar

Monk Bar from within. There are two chambers above the central arch which were used in the sixteenth century as a prison. Through the bar, the second St Maurice's church built in 1878 and demolished in 1967, can be seen.

Monk Bar is the highest of four bars. The figures at the top are hurling stones – not exactly a welcome gesture for those entering the city through this gateway! The side arches were added in the nineteenth century to allow hay carts easier access into the city and the barbican was removed in 1825.

The portcullis at Monk Bar lowered, 1914. The machinery used to raise the portcullis is kept in the top storey of the bar. It is the only hoisting mechanism to survive in York.

Plane Tree Court, St Maurice's Road c. 1926. The Groves in the shadow of the walls between Monk Bar and Clarence Street was a residential area in which all the social classes were represented. This row of back-to-back terraces housed the poorest of the community. The block of communal privies can be seen.

These houses in Jackson Street, curiously numbered $16\frac{1}{2}$, $17\frac{1}{2}$, $18\frac{1}{2}$ and $19\frac{1}{2}$, with their own walled or railed gardens were probably inhabited by the better off among the working classes.

Lords Mayor's Walk contained smarter terraces. Among the occupations of those living in the road listed in the 1900 directory, were a verger at the Minster, a watchmaker and a valuer. William Hayes who took this photograph and many of the others in this book, had lived around the corner in St John's Street and probably knew many of the people posing here.

An unexpected sight, sheep belonging to Reynolds Farm, graze in the moat along Lord Mayor's Walk.

Incredibly, this seemingly rural scene is Reynolds Farm on the corner of Gillygate and Lord Mayors Walk. It was taken as recently as 1957.

Monk Bridge before it was widened between 1924-26. Its humped shape was necessary for the boats using the Foss Navigation but was an obstacale for horse-drawn vehicles which sometimes needed extra assistance to get across the bridge.

The John Bull photographed in 1935. It was rebuilt on an adjoining site in 1937 with a Tudor style exterior and remained unchanged inside until it was closed in May 1994, in the face of vigorous public opposition.

Redeness Street is typical of the rows of terracing that were crammed into Layerthorpe. It was one of the few areas of extreme poverty with narrow, dingy streets and small, dark houses that had grown up outside the city walls.

Layerthorpe Infant School, St Cuthbert's Road in the 1920s. It was opened to ease the overcrowding at Bilton Street School, an indication of the general overcrowding in the Layerthorpe area.

The Layerthorpe branch of the York Co-operative Society. The co-ops gave a lifeline to those living on the poverty line, especially when it came to the time for collecting the divvy! With stores throughout the city and suburbs, its membership grew from 7,250 in 1900 to 22,820 in 1940.

The premises of J. H. Walker, builders and coal merchants, on Layerthorpe Bridge 1928. The business continued from here until 1973 when they moved to Foss Island Road where they are still to be found today. Layerthorpe beyond was dominated by the gasworks. Originally only on

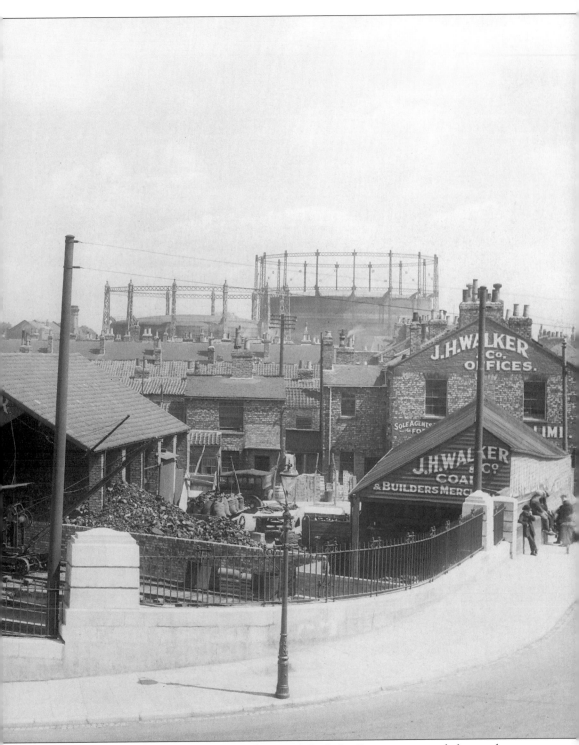

the west bank of the River Foss, the York United Gaslight Company expanded onto the east
bank between 1879 and 1881 and the new works were built in the early 1880s.

First Avenue, Heworth complete with railings along both sides of the street.

The York Union Workhouse, on Huntington Road opened in 1848 and was built to accommodate 300 inmates at a cost of £6,000. It attempted to keep its occupants busy with a carpentry shop, school of industry and oakum room, where the menial task of unravelling ropes took place. It became The Grange and later St. Mary's Hospital and can still be seen today.

Workers leaving Rowntree's factory for lunch in the 1950s. They are mainly women and this is borne out in the statistics: of a total female workforce in the city of about 18,000 in 1951 approximately 5,100 worked in the confectionery industry, whereas the chief employer of men was the railways.

The tuberculosis wards at Yearsley Bridge Infectious Diseases Hospital, Huntington Road where the emphasis was placed on the healing powers of fresh air! The hospital opened in June 1881, with the tuberculosis wards added in 1912, and it continued treating patients until its closure in December 1976.

A group of patients and staff from Yearsley Bridge Hospital in 1920. The gentleman on the right receiving medicine from the nurse, recovered from the consumption that had hospitalised him and is still alive and well today.

Seven
Through Micklegate Bar

Micklegate Bar from Blossom Street when both Nunnery Lane and Queen Street were narrow roads leading from it.

St Thomas' Hospital adjoining what is now The Punch Bowl. Founded in 1391, It was demolished in 1860 after conditions were reported to be damp and dark, and rebuilt further down Nunnery Lane. The building here now is The Moat Hotel. Its disappearance considerably widened the entrance to this street.

A view down Queens Street before it was widened in 1907 for the advent of electric trams. York's first station was situated here. Always intended to be temporary, it was used from 1839 until 1841 when the station in Toft Green was opened.

A bird's eye view of the terraces off Holgate Road with St Paul's Church in the distance, 1937. These tightly-packed streets were built to accommodate the railway workers. A clearance order was served on the area in 1937 and they were eventually demolished in the 1960s. Denton Terrace, the back of Mount Ephriam and Stafford Place are in the foreground.

Mount Ephraim, Holgate Road. The name still survives but today's street is not recognisable from this picture.

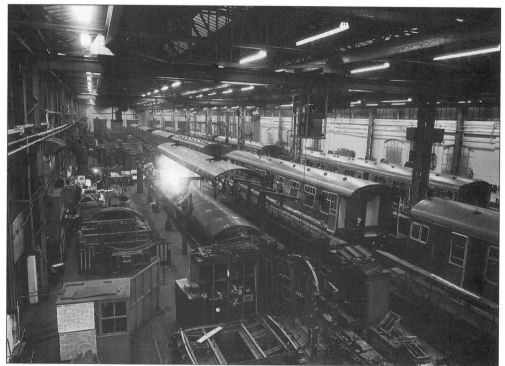

The carriage building shop. The carriage works, Holgate Road, 1964. The train-building began in Holgate in 1865. Over the next century, the original workshops were continually extended so that by 1958, the site covered 62 acres. Sadly, over recent years, this expansion has been reversed and the workforce has gradually been slimmed down. The last trains to be made in Holgate are currently being produced and the works close in December 1995, ending a long tradition.

The Fox, Holgate Road, c. 1885. There has been an inn on this site since the 1770s. It became known as The Fox in 1845 and these premises were built in 1878.

Holgate Mill, 1911. The miller who lived here from 1902 to 1924 was Herbert Warters and it is probably him in the picture. During his time, the mill was still producing white and brown flour, but after 1924 it fell into partial disuse. His successor was Thomas Mollett, the last miller, who had left by 1936, signalling the end of the mill's working life.

Holgate Windmill from the Grantham Drive end of Windmill Rise, c. 1940. It is a smock mill and its unusual feature of five sails stand out dramatically in this photograph.

White Row Cottages, Front Street, Acomb. Today it is difficult to picture Acomb as a rural village. However Kelly's 1889 West Riding Directory describes it as a place where the soil is chiefly sandy and the main crops are wheat, barley, turnip and seeds. This row of cottages was modernised in the 1920s and more recently the central one has been replaced to allow access to Chancellor's Court, a new housing development which stands behind them.

Front Street, Acomb. On the right a shopkeeper stands outside one of the purpose built shops along the street, 1900. They included a draper, tobacconist and confectioner, a hairdresser, grocer, and toy and fancy goods dealer.

Beaconsfield Street, 1890s. Acomb's population rapidly increased in the late 1800s, rising from 963 in 1871 to 2,181 in 1891. The housing development in and around Beaconsfield Street and also in the Carr Lane area was built to accommodate this expansion, which was partly due to the larger workforce required by the growing carriage works.

Frank Carlill's grocery, provisions store and greengrocers in Beaconsfield Street served Acomb for over eighty years. His son, Arthur, left school during the First World War to help manage his father's business and was a managing director from 1933 until his retirement in 1969. Now Arthur's son, another Frank, runs the Post Office at the bottom of Holgate Hill.

Ouseburn Avenue was built by Ouseburn Rural District Council. The estate contained 116 houses and these were the only council houses in Acomb when it became part of York in 1937.

Maypole dancing on Acomb Green.

The Regent Cinema, Acomb Road in 1955. It entertained the people of Acomb from 1934 to 1959, boasting the largest screen of any in the York suburbs and double seats on the back row!

Scarcroft Road from Bishopthorpe Road is a scene where little has changed over the years, apart from the felling of the tree in front of St Clement's church and the absence of cars!

Bishopthorpe Road at the Scarcroft Road Junction, looking towards Clementhorpe and Bishopgate Street. In 1889, roughly the time of this photograph, housing down Bishopthorpe Road had only reached as far as Southlands Methodist Chapel on one side and Richardson Street on the other. Beyond this were open fields.

Eight

Transport

A motor bus performs a dangerous manoeuvre in Museum Street in 1934. It is passing an electric tramcar which is itself passing a stationary motor car.

York's second station opened in 1877, after the original station in Toft Green was no longer able to cope with increasing volume of traffic. This larger station has been described as a 'cathedral of civil engineering' and its grandeur reflected York's importance as a railway town.

The interior of York Station, c. 1880. The magnificence of the curved roof is evident in this photograph. The footbridge has not yet been erected and passengers used two subways to cross the line, both of which are still in use today.

A steam locomotive at the platform at the end of York Station 1912-1914. It is a North Eastern Railway Class Z, 3-cylinder 4-4-2. They were built between 1911 and 1918 and continued to run until the Second World War.

The opening of the new and enlarged lock at Naburn by the Duke of Clarence and the Lord Mayor Alderman Rymer in 1888. The first lock had been constructed in 1757 and did much to improve the navigation of the River Ouse but was not big enough for the boats which used the river in the next century.

York Corporation began a programme of providing an electric tramway system in 1909. In this view, the men are laying the tramlines along Station Avenue in 1909-1910 as routes leaving and entering the city from the south had to go past the station to avoid Micklegate.

York's first electric tram ran from Fulford to the city centre and the service was opened in January 1910 by the Lord Mayor Alderman Birch. With him is driver Stewart who also drove the last tramcar in 1935. Here the celebratory journey has reached Clifford Street. The tramways were a feature of the city until they closed in November 1935 giving way to the greater flexibility of the motor buses.

A trolley bus from Heworth arrives in Pavement in 1921, shortly after the line opened in December 1920. This form of transport was chosen for Heworth to avoid the expensive street works required for the tramcars and was in use until 1935.

An impressive array of cars for sale at Leedhams in Tanner's Moat, c. 1935-36. The firm was established in 1924 and continues to serve York motorists today.

This car belongs to Dr Alfred Waugh Metcalfe of St Leonard's Place. It is 'driven' here by Kenneth Greenwood outside The Gables in Sycamore Place and the photograph is dated 1910. According to the records, in 1910, Dr Metcalfe had a three-seater red Sideley, registered DN26.

York Motor Club meet outside the Minster in c. 1904. Car registration began in 1904 with all those registered in York given the prefix 'DN'. DN2, left of centre, was the second car to be registered and belonged to Alfred Jackson of Albemarle House in Clifford Street. It was a 4.5 Horsepower DeDion black and yellow Voiturette. DN15 on the extreme left, is a two seater with a yellow body owned by Harry Reynolds of St Saviourgate.

Rawcliffe Lane Aerodrome, 1938. It was opened by York Corporation as a municipal airfield on 4 July 1936.

A view of Rawcliffe Lane Aerodrome from the top of a newly-erected hanger. The planes refuelling at the pumps are Gypsy 1 Moths. During World War Two, the airfield was enlarged for Royal Air Force use.

The Fenton Zip Tandem complete with the Fenton Zip Sidecar is ridden by its inventor F.W. Fenton and his wife, who were both members of the Clifton Cycling Club. It is regarded by many as the best of its kind ever produced. The aerodynamic sidecar was designed by craftsmen from the aircraft works Airspeed Ltd based in Piccadilly.

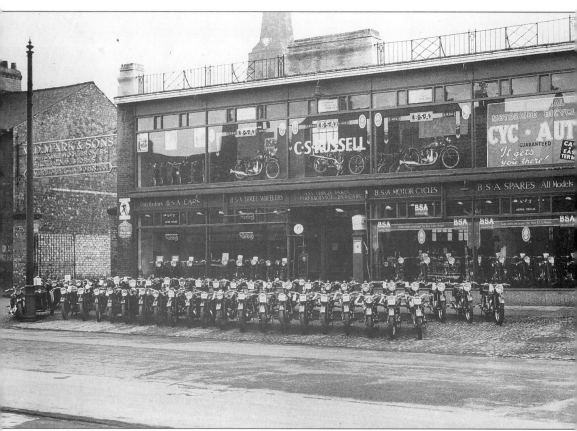

C. S. Russell, Motorcycle dealers, Lawrence Street, 1937. Established in 1904, by 1929 Russell's had two outlets in York, this one and their city centre store on the corner of Coppergate and Clifford Street. They catered for all York's biking needs until 1986 when the motorcycle department closed, but continue to serve pedal cyclists from their new shop in Toft Green.

Nine
At Leisure

York City Rowing Club at their 'At home regatta', c. 1948. It always took place at the end of the season and judging by the number of trophies on display, this one had been a rather successful one!

A passerby stops in Clifford Street to plan his social life by perusing the advertising hoardings in 1902. They were a common sight in York, and elsewhere, until they were brought under control by the 1948 Town and Country Planning Act.

The Black Bull Hotel, Finkle Street, 1905. Judging by the number of pubs in York, drinking is and has always been, one of the main leisure activities of its citizens! The lantern hanging outside the door states that it has a Music Hall, an additional attraction to tempt people inside, in the face of competition from the large number of inns in the marketplace.

The Theatre Royal, Exhibition Square. There has been a theatre on this site since 1744. The canopy in this photograph has since been removed to reveal the Victorian Gothic front which was put in by the city engineer in 1880 for the theatre's owner W. A. Waddington. The award-winning cafe area replaced the brick scene dock to the left of the theatre in 1967.

The Picture House, Coney Street, 1940. It opened in April 1915 and cost £10,000 to build. Its internal decoration was very luxurious with oak panelling and an ornate ceiling in the entrance hall, but it was a victim of the rising waters of the Ouse during the periodic floods. As the levels rose, rows of seats in the auditorium were cordoned off! It closed in 1955and the site was acquired by Woolworths.

The Rialto, Fishergate, 1929-1935. Initially called the City Picture Palace, it was built between 1908 and 1909 but by 1929, was known as The Rialto. It was destroyed by fire in April 1935 and a second Rialto, which we see today, rose from the ashes. The Beatles appeared here in 1963.

St George's Hall Cinema, Castlegate opened in March 1921 with seating for 1,340 people. It was entered through the building next door to Fairfax House which was itself used as a ballroom. The cinema closed in November 1965 and the auditorium was demolished.

The Knavesmire, which belonged to the Freemen of York, has been home to the York races since 1731. It is also enjoyed as an open space for a number of other activities. Football, cricket, jogging and kite-flying all take place regularly as well as more organized events like firework displays, fairs and hot air balloon launches. In this picture a family enjoys a picnic c. 1905.

In 1926 York racecorse was used for a Mission organized by this group of Wesleyans.

A game of cricket underway on Acomb Green. As early as 1843, the Green was seen as the cricket pitch for the village and the present Acomb Cricket Club stands only a stones throw away from it.

The York City Football Team that reached the FA Cup quarter finals in 1938. In this famous cup run, they knocked out two first division sides, West Bromwich Albion in the fourth round and Middlesborough in the fifth round, before losing to Huddersfield in a replay. Their giant-killing exploits continue today, most recently with victory over Manchester United in the League Cup in September 1995.

York R.L. v. Dewsbury 'Scrummage under the posts'. The exact date of this game is unknown though it is thought it be soon after the Clarence Street ground opened. It is believed to be the earliest photograph of a game on this pitch.

Clifton Cycling Club pose here in their foundation year, 1895. The club is still thriving today.

Clifton Cycling Club, 1937, setting off on their Sunday ride from Exhibition Square, their regular meeting place since 1896.

Three quarters of the Team Time Trial Team representing Great Britain at the 1968 Olympics were from Clifton Cycling Club. Here they pose in their official ties and blazers ready to set off from Clifton for Mexico City. From left to right are Pete Smith, John Watson and Roy Cromick. The fourth member of the team was a Scotsman.

CLARENCE GARDENS BOWLING CLUB YORK 5 AUG 12

The swimming baths in Rowntree's Park which were open air and unheated. The park was presented to the City in 1921 by the Rowntree family and the baths were opened in 1924. They closed in 1980 but live on in the memories of the many York people who used them.

Opposite: Clarence Gardens Bowling club, 5 August 1912. All members are in their Sunday best with buttonholes and highly polished shoes! Among them are Walter Iddison (second row, third left) whose uncle was Roger Iddison, the Yorkshire Cricket captain and all-rounder, and J. Baines whose father was Reg Baines, the York City footballer.

York and Ainsty Hunt outside The Sun Inn, Acomb. The hunt was established in 1816 and covered the area from Thirsk in the North to Selby in the South and from Howden in the East to Pateley Bridge in the West. The hounds were kennelled on Foxwood Lane until they were demolished in 1972. The *Bystander* magazine, describing the hounds in 1909, stated that 'the bitches are a good-looking, hard-driving lot, though the dogs are somewhat wanting in dash and are by no means equal to the lady pack in perserverance and drive'!

Ten

Dramas

The fire at Leak & Thorp on 23 January 1933 was so serious that the decision was made to evacuate the city centre. The fire could be seen for miles around with the aid of a strong North Westerly wind. The firm moved into premises in Lendal while their new shop in Coney Street was built. It reopened in September 1934.

It took the combined forces of the Corporation and Rowntree's Cocoa Works fire brigades more than six hours to bring the fire at Boyes on 8 December 1910 under control. A large crowd gathered to watch their endeavours. The six-storey building was completely gutted and had to be pulled down. A new store was built, reopening in July 1912.

The internal devastation wreaked by the Boyes blaze. The fire started in the toy department when Christmas decorations came into contact with gas lamps.

On the 1 February 1912 while the new Boyes store was being constructed the clock tower collapsed and fell through to the basement, killing one workman and injuring seven others. It was never rebuilt. Instead, a clock was put in the front of the building overlooking Bridge Street.

Boyes in the process of rebuilding, June 1912. The total cost of the new store was just over £6,500 and it used reinforced concrete – a very new form of construction at this time. Here the men are testing its strength by loading with bricks.

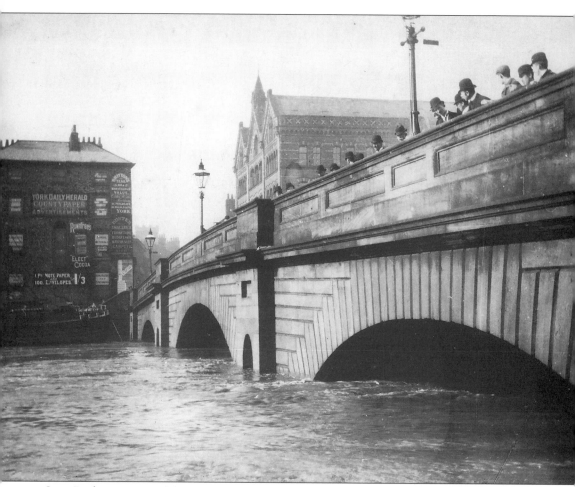

Ouse Bridge, 1892. York has always been at the mercy of the River Ouse with the water rising at a rapid rate as it leaves the higher ground around the Vale of York. Here passers by watch as the flood waters sweep by almost reaching the top of the arches.

Hetherton Street in 1947 when the Ouse rose to 16 ft 4½ inches. Hetherton Street and Walker Street below stood where St Mary's car park is now.

Walker Street, 1947. Its residents are rescued by horse and cart, a form of transport which did not run the risk of becoming waterlogged as motor vehicles then did.

North Street, here in 1947, is among the first roads to become flooded when the Ouse breaks its banks. Its vulnerability was recognised in 1992 when work started on a flood barrier which has so far proved effective.

No. 33 North Street during the 1931 flood. Mr and Mrs Press stand on a swiftly erected walkway above the flood water. Francis Press had a greengrocers in North Street where his family lived for several generations.

Excavating the Roman Fortress walls in the 1930s near Monk Bar. Digs are always dramatic occasions in York, as you can never be sure what treasures may be waiting to be unearthed.

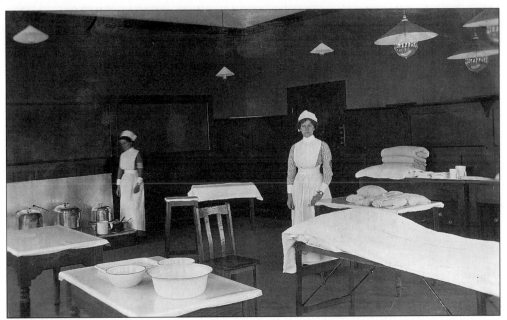

The Mount School, Dalton Terrace is prepared as a hospital for the wounded of World War One in August 1914. However, the wounded never arrived and the school regained its buildings with term starting only a fortnight later.

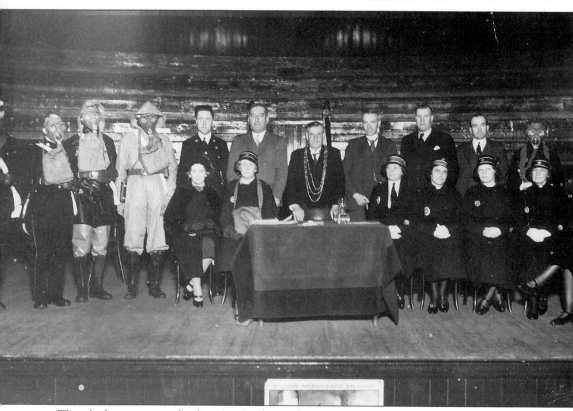

The platform party at the first Air Raid Patrol meeting in Exhibition Buildings on 5 February 1937, presided over by Lord Mayor Alderman Thomas Morris. Gas masks seem to have been viewed as a novel item as early as 1937, with several members of the party keen to wear them for this photograph!

The Guildhall, Coney Street, April 1942. One of the most historic casualties of the Baedeker Raid on York on 29 April 1942 was the medieval guildhall. A City Council memo of September 1944 states that all the interior oak woodwork had been destroyed by incendiary bombs landing on the decks of scaffolding that had been erected to repair the ravages of the death watch beetle. To replace it required 'ten whole trees of very large dimensions'. The estimated cost of rebuilding to the original design was £50,000.

Holgate Ward Air Raid patrol unit stands outside the warden's post on Poppleton Road. These men witnessed action on the night of the Baedeker Raid when Poppleton Road School received a direct hit and Lavender Grove, Plantation Drive, Chatsworth Terrace, Amberly Street, Malvern Avenue and Manor Drive were all damaged by high explosives.

Although the Baedeker Raid is the most famous, there were ten other air strikes on York during World War Two. This is Sefton Avenue, which along with Elmfield Avenue, was bombed on 29 October 1940. Two people were killed and the photograph shows the devastation that ordinary householders suffered. Nine and half thousand houses were damaged during the raids of 1939-1945.

No. 204 Beckfield Lane, Acomb 15 November 1940. In this raid, there were two serious casualties, some animals were killed and there was damage to houses and factories.

Eleven

Celebrations
and Ceremonies

York Fine Art and Industrial Exhibition was held from 24 July until 31 October 1866 on Bootham Asylum Fields. The building took four months to assemble and only one month to dismantle! The event attracted 337,881 visitors and was partly a showcase for the local tradesmen to promote their businesses. Among the many York firms represented were Kilvington wire manufactures, Leak & Thorp furnishings and Thomas Cooke instrument makers who supplied a clock.

The interior of the York Fine Art and Industrial Exhibition, 1866, showing the Great Hall which was 195 feet long and 80 ft wide and where the industrial part of the exhibition was displayed. Running above this were the picture galleries. They contained paintings by the great masters loaned from private collections around the county and works by contemporary artists. Other rooms included a small natural history exhibition area, a lecture room and first and second class refreshment rooms!

Among the visitors to the 1866 exhibition were Their Royal Highnesses the Prince and Princess of Wales. This arch on Ouse Bridge, along with others throughout the city, were erected in their honour.

Another highlight of the 1866 exhibition was a review on the Knavesmire of the North of England Volunteers by the Duke of Cambridge in the presence of the Prince and Princess of Wales.

The Mystery Plays, Museum Gardens, 1951. This was the first time the cycle had been performed since 1572. It was decided to revive it as part of York's contribution to the Festival of Britain. The cast was drawn mainly from the local community, including Judy Dench playing an angel and Mary Ure who went on to appear in *Where Eagles Dare* in 1968.

The York Historic Pageant took place in July 1909 and was a re-enactment in seven episodes of major events in York's history, beginning in 800 BC. York's was the last of six that had taken place around the country, with the first held in Sherbourne in 1905. Here a procession passes down Museum Street through a Roman arch erected for the occasion.

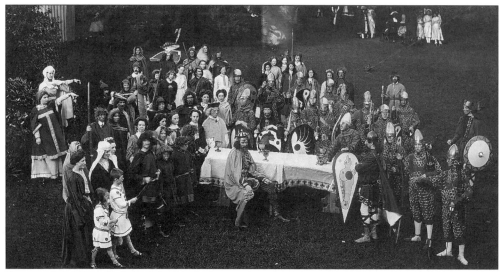

A scene from episode five of the York Historic Pageant 1909 in which King Stephen arrives in the city following the Battle of the Standard in 1138. Over two thousand performers took part in the event, with many more involved behind the scenes. The finale was a magnificent tableau and chorus singing the *Triumph Song of York*.

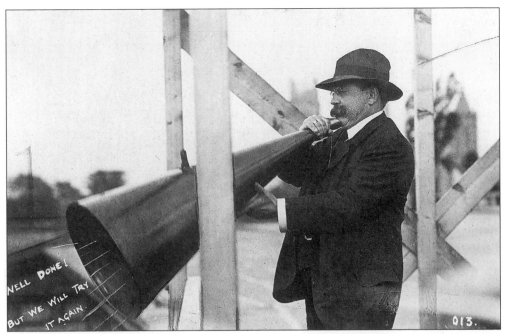

Louis Napolean Parker, Pageant Master at the York Historical Pageant in 1909. He had officiated at all the other pageants around the country and during performances directed proceedings from his crows nest above the grandstand. In his autobiography, he gives a special mention to Dorothy B. Ramsay, later Mrs H. A. Wilson, writing 'I would not have got through the York pageant if it had not been for her wise and sympathetic guidance'!

Crowds celebrate Queen Victoria's Diamond Jubilee in 1897 in Exhibition Square outside Bootham Bar.

The Duke of York, later George V, on a visit to York, travelling down the Mount on 19 June 1900. He was on his way to join his father at the Royal Agricultural Show on the Knavesmire. The lack of spectators lining the road contrasts with the crowds in the scene below.

The Queen visits York in 1971. Nuns and pupils at The Bar Convent endeavour to catch a glimpse of the royal coach as it travels down Blossom Streen and through Micklegate Bar. Some peer out of the windows, while the lucky ones are seated on the wide window ledges.

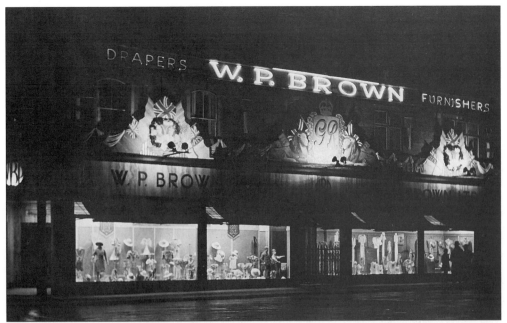

W.P. Browns in St Sampson's Square decorated for the coronation in 1937.

Unveiling the the George Leeman Statue on Station Rise 13 April 1885. It was sculpted by the York sculptor, Milburn in his studio near Bootham Bar. The ceremony was held at noon to allow what the newspaper describes as the 'working classes' to attend and from the size of the crowd, it looks like many took the opportunity.

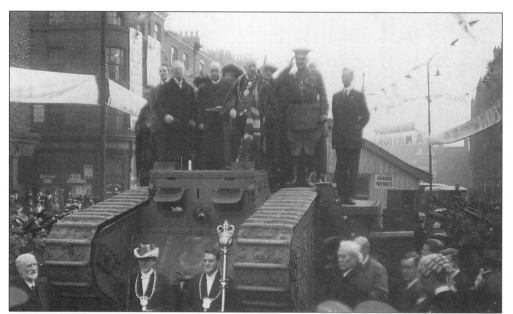

The opening of Tank Week on 16 February 1918 by the Lord Mayor Alderman Forster-Todd. 'Nelson' the tank, was on a tour of the country to urge people to contribute to the war effort by buying war savings and bonds. Civic pride and competitive spirit were called on by the Lord Mayor to encourage York to raise more than Bradford had in the previous week, which meant reaching a total figure of £1,000,000.

Millfield Road in August 1918 decorated for a street party to celebrate the peace at the end of The Great War. One of the events planned was a children's fancy dress competition.

The official opening of Skeldergate Bridge on 10 March 1881 was a cause for celebration in the city. Parliamentary permission to construct the bridge was granted in 1875 and a much earlier completion date had been anticipated. In his address, the Lord Mayor put the delay down to difficulties with the foundations in the river bed and the inclemency of the weather.

Freeing Skeldergate Bridge from tolls on 1 April 1914. The construction of the bridge had cost about £50,000, a far larger sum than had been expected. However the volume of traffic using the bridge was such that in just over thirty years the tolls were abandoned.

York Hospital, Saturday 1905. Despite appearances, this photograph was taken in July! The float was part of the Hospital Saturday Parade which had started in 1901 as a money raising event for the hospital.